# Max and the Magical Yoga Forest

By S.G. Bloomfield

Illustrated by: Kate Chirko

Max and the Magical Yoga Forest




First Edition: 2023

Design and layout by Stefania Grieco

Published by Stefania Grieco

Hardcover ISBN: 978-1-7380274-1-5

Paperback ISBN: 978-1-7380274-0-8

E-book ISBN: 978-1-7380274-2-2

To the dreamers, the adventurers, and the young at heart,

This tale is woven for you. Within its pages, discover a realm where wonder and stillness intertwine. Just as Max ventured into the heart of the magical forest, know that your own heart is a treasure trove of enchantments waiting to be uncovered.

As you journey with every turn of the page, may your spirit find its rhythm, and may the pulse of the forest echo in your every heartbeat. Even when the last word is read, let the magic linger - in every mindful moment, every breath, and every shared smile.

Embrace the adventure, find your center, and let the universe's wonders envelop you.

To the magic that dwells both in the unseen and seen, but most importantly, to you — the bearers of endless magic.

With warmth, wonder, and a touch of whimsy,

S.G. Bloomfield

One sunny day, Max was reading a book about magical creatures and enchanted forests.

He wondered what it would be like to visit such a fascinating place.

Max's mom saw
his excitement
and decided to
share a new
yoga book
with him.

The book was called "Max and the Magical Yoga Forest,"
and it captured Max's imagination.

As Max and his mom read the book,
the magical forest came to life.

There were colorful trees, sparkling water, and friendly animals that practiced yoga together.

In his imagination, Max stepped into the magical forest and met a wise owl who offered to teach him new yoga poses.

Max and the wise owl practiced the Butterfly Pose together, surrounded by a beautiful garden filled with flowers and butterflies.

The playful dolphin taught Max the Dolphin Pose,
as he balanced on his forearms and
lifted his hips high in the crystal-clear pond.

Max and a strong bear practiced the Bear Crawl Pose together, crawling along the soft, mossy forest floor and feeling his muscles grow stronger.

With a group of elegant flamingos,
Max practiced the Flamingo Pose,
balancing on one leg by
the side of a peaceful lake.

In a peaceful glade, Max and the wise owl practiced mindfulness and meditation, focusing on this breath and the sounds of the magical forest.

Soon, Max's friends from school joined him in
the magical forest, eager to learn new yoga poses
from the wise owl and the other friendly animals.

Max and his friends practiced
the Star Pose together,

spreading their arms and legs wide, gazing up at the sky filled with twinkling stars.

The children sat in a circle with the wise owl, practicing deep breathing and listening to the gentle sounds of the magical forest, feeling connected to nature and each other.

Max and his friends said goodbye to the wise owl and the magical animals, promising to return and practice yoga together again soon.

Max and his friends stepped out of the magical forest and back into their everyday lives, feeling refreshed, strong, and balanced, carrying the magic of the forest with them.

Max and his mom
shared a warm hug,
grateful for his shared experience
in the magical yoga forest
and the lessons he learned
from his new friends.

With a peaceful smile on his face,
Max gazed out the window of his room,
knowing that the magical yoga forest
was always there for him whenever
he needed it, just a breath
and a stretch away.

The End

# Magical Yoga Forest Explorations: Join Max on a bonus journey!

# Max's Mystical Forest Labyrinth

Help Max navigate the Magical Yoga Forest! Start at the entrance and find your way to the wise old owl in the center. Use a pencil or crayon to trace your path without crossing any tree lines. Good luck!

# Max's Magical Word Hunt

Find the words listed above in the puzzle. Circle or highlight each word as you find it. Enjoy and have fun!

R G
H C G P O R B Y
D N W R A E B R J
N O Y C V U X A M Y Z V
V K I W W V N F L Y U D
X G V T B N L F D F F J W
F A L D G H A R N U O S W X
M S A P W M E U B A R A P L
E V M T S I T W Y Q K E C S
A T K N T D V G O D S C S
Y G U B B C W D G T J W
O B O I P D E N W A J
W X L W O U I L
S Z O
T
W T A
Y R Q S R
D V Q C J
Z V V S F I
R O W G L
I Z A
Y J R E E G R Y L
Y B W S N I H P L O D
D V E T M O Y

Max

Yoga

Forest

Owl

Butterfly

Dolphin

Bear

Flamingo

Star

Magic

## Hints:

Longer words are often easier to spot than shorter ones.

Words might be hidden diagonally, not just up and down or side to side.

If you can't find a word, try looking at the puzzle from different angles

# Max's Enchanted Forest Clues Quest

1. Match clues to story words.
2. Fill in across and down.
3. Some letters are shared.
4. Enjoy the puzzle fun! 🌳 🔍 🖊️

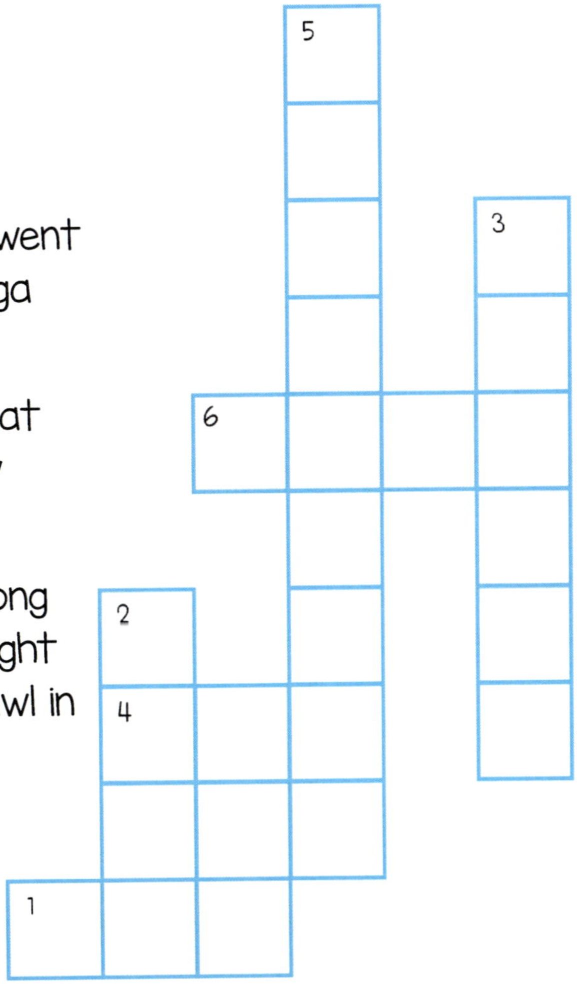


Across:

1. The main character who went on a magical yoga adventure.

4. A wise bird that taught Max new poses.

6. A big and strong animal that taught Max how to crawl in the forest.

Down:

2. A practice of poses and breathing that helps you feel calm and strong.

3. A large area covered with trees where Max's magical journey took place.

5. An insect with colorful wings; also a pose Max learned.

# Max's Mystical Image Mix

Place each image (Owl, Dolphin, Max, Flamingo) in every row, column, and box. No image should repeat in any row, column, or box. Happy puzzling!

# Enchanted Creature Craft

Imagine a new magical animal for the Yoga Forest. Draw it, name it, and decide which yoga pose it teaches Max. Let your imagination soar!

# Max's Enchanted Forest Tranquility

This meditation is designed for both children and adults to foster a sense of peace and connection with nature. Before we begin, find a quiet spot where you won't be disturbed. Sit or lie down in a comfortable position, and let's embark on a magical journey together.

Close your eyes and take a deep, calming breath. Let go of any other thoughts and just focus on your breathing. Feel your chest rise as you breathe in, and feel it fall as you breathe out.

Now, imagine you're standing at the entrance of the magical yoga forest. The sky is painted in soft pastel colors from the setting sun, and there's a gentle, welcoming glow coming from the trees ahead.

With every step you take into the forest, you feel the soft grass under your feet. The world outside starts to fade away, replaced by the enchanting world of the forest. The trees seem to sway slightly, greeting you as old friends would.

You hear the distant sound of water flowing. It's the crystal-clear pond where the playful dolphins practice their poses. Can you hear their joyous splashes and see the ripples on the water's surface?

Walking further, the gentle hum of the forest surrounds you. Birds are softly chirping in the canopy above, and the rustling of the leaves seems to sync with your heartbeat.

You soon find a cozy spot, surrounded by a bed of flowers and a canopy of trees. Taking a seat, you feel the energy of the forest infusing you with calmness and peace. It's as if the forest is sharing its age-old wisdom with you.

Breathe in deeply, soaking in the fresh forest air, filled with the scent of pine and blooming flowers. As you exhale, let go of any remaining tension, and imagine roots growing from your body, connecting you to the earth, grounding you.

The wise owl from Max's adventure might be perched on a branch nearby, its eyes full of understanding and warmth. You're not alone in this forest; you're surrounded by friendly, magical creatures, all here to share in this moment of peace with you.

Stay in this moment for as long as you like. When you're ready to return, start by wiggling your fingers and toes. Gently bring your awareness back to your surroundings, but carry the magic and serenity of the forest with you.

Open your eyes slowly, holding onto the feeling of connection and tranquility. Remember, the magical yoga forest is always there for you, just a thought and a breath away.

# Whimsical Woodland Yoga Journal

Draw or write about your yoga pose experiences. Did you feel strong, graceful, or something else? Share your forest yoga adventure here!

# Mindfulness Coloring Page

Find a quiet and comfortable spot. As you color in the picture of Max and their friends practicing yoga, take deep breaths and focus on the present moment. Notice the colors and textures of the coloring page, and enjoy the process of creating a beautiful scene

Dear Magical Adventurer,

We've come to the end of our enchanted journey, and what a radiant path it has been! Through the mystical mazes of the forest, the word hunts filled with secrets, and the puzzles that unlocked the magic within, you've truly embodied the spirit of the forest and yoga.

Every step, every stretch, every breath you took wasn't just a mere activity. You were connecting to your inner self, understanding nature, and embracing the wisdom that yoga brings. Your dedication and zest to dive into these pages warmed our hearts and showed us the bright spark within you.

Remember, life is a lot like our journey through this book. There may be challenges that seem twisted and turns that might confuse, but with patience, breath, and a bit of magic, you can find your way and shine bright.

Thank you for embracing this magical yoga adventure with such enthusiasm. This might be the end of this book, but it's just the beginning of your unique, enchanted journey. There's a vast world out there, waiting to be explored through stretches, breaths, and dreams.

Keep stretching, keep dreaming, and keep believing in the magic within you. We're cheering you on every step of the way and can't wait to meet you again on another mystical journey.

Stay Magical and Keep Breathing,
With love and light from the enchanted forest. 🌟🧘🌟

# SOLUTIONS

# Sudoku Solution

# Word Search Solution

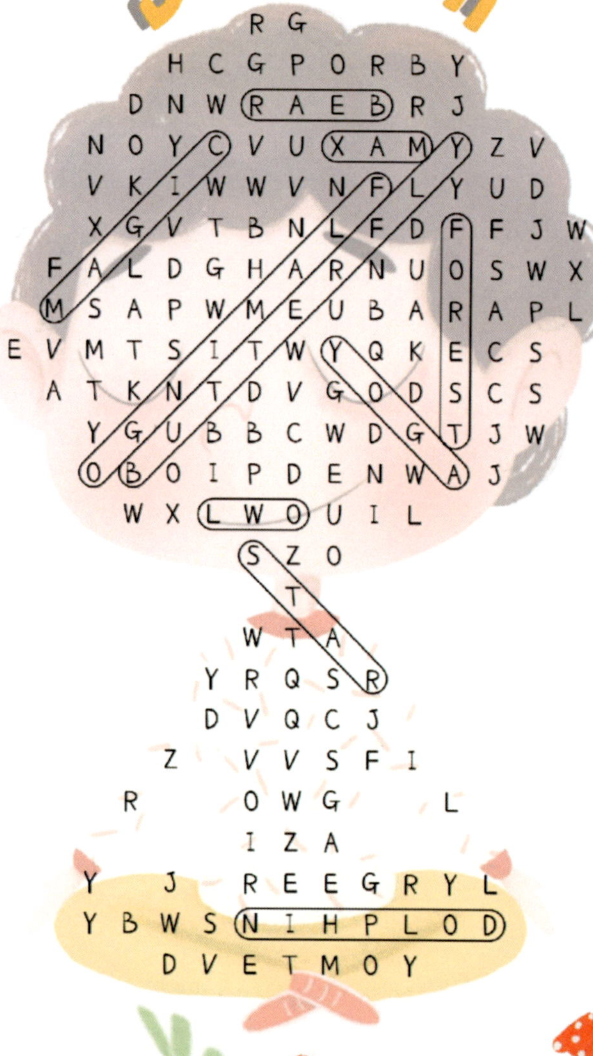

# CrossWord Solution

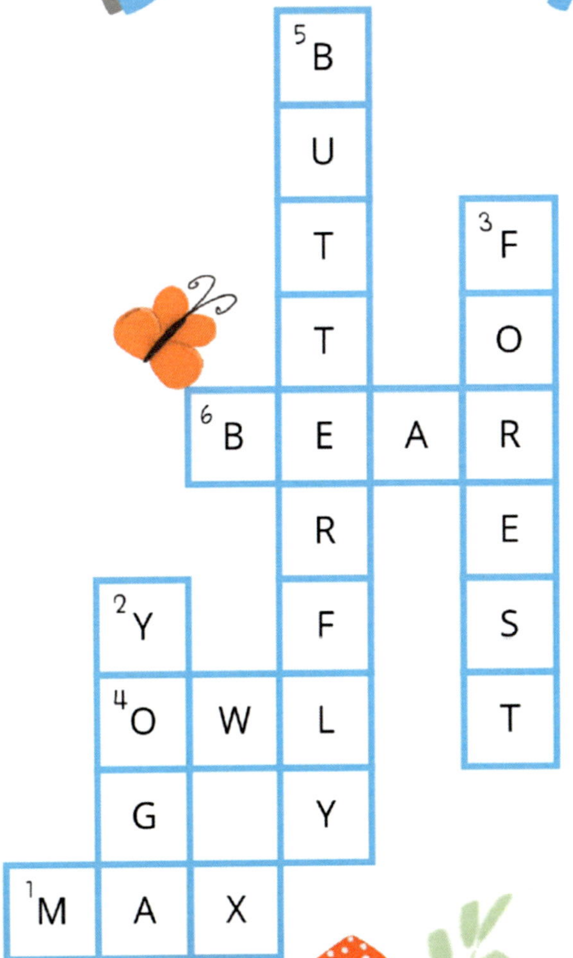


# Maze Solution

# About the Author page

About the Author: S.G. Bloomfield is a self-taught artist and registered yoga instructor who is passionate about sharing the benefits of yoga and mindfulness with people of all ages. Born and raised in Canada, S.G. Bloomfield currently resides in Belize, Central America. After completing their yoga teacher training on November 11, 2017, they were fortunate enough to teach Kid yoga and Puppy yoga at the same yoga studio where they trained. In addition to the Little Yogi series, S.G. Bloomfield has also written a guide for adults, helping them embrace their inner light through the practice of yoga. They are the owner, designer, artist, and photographer behind Home Time Art, an Etsy shop offering modern, minimalist, nursery, spiritual, and yoga high-quality printable art as instant downloads. S.G. Bloomfield is dedicated to providing unique, personalized designs that bring joy and beauty to people's lives.

# About the Illustrator page

Kate Chirko is a Ukrainian artist and illustrator whose true passion lies in creating enchanting illustrations for children. With a focus on children's books, Kate's delightful and whimsical paintings are loved by both young readers and adults alike. Fluent in conversational English, she effortlessly brings stories to life through her incredible attention to detail and innate artistic talent. Using tools like Photoshop and Procreate, Kate's skills are truly impressive. Clients from around the world are drawn to her work and often return for more, captivated by her ability to capture the essence of a story. Kate Chirko is hailed as an amazing artist, leaving customers thoroughly delighted with their experience. Connect with her on Facebook and Dribbble using her handle, @katechirko, to witness her remarkable illustrations that will transport you to a world of imagination and wonder.

# Dive into the Little Yogi Adventures!

"**<u>The Little Yogi</u>**"

After a challenging day at school, young Max discovers the transformative world of yoga and mindfulness with the help of a special book and their caring mom. As Max learns and practices various poses, not only does their confidence grow, but they also become a beacon of peace and understanding at school. This heartwarming tale highlights the impact of inner strength, kindness, and the timeless lessons of the Little Yogi.

Available now! Dive into the magical journey with Max and discover the world of yoga, mindfulness, and friendship. Grab your copy today!

# More Adventures Await!

Get ready for more exciting stories with Max and their friends as they continue to explore the world of yoga, mindfulness, and friendship in our upcoming Little Yogi series. Here's a sneak peek at what's to come:

"**The Yuletide Yogi**"
Journey with Max to a winter wonderland where yoga unveils holiday magic. Amidst snow and festive spirits, Max learns unique poses, embraces mindfulness, and bonds with mystical creatures. Dive into this yuletide adventure and stretch your imagination!

"**Max and the Mindful Moon**"
Max brings the joy of yoga and mindfulness to their community by hosting a unique Mindful Moon Festival. Alongside friends, they create an enchanting night of yoga, meditation, and activities that unite everyone under the moonlit sky.

Stay tuned for these exciting new stories and more. We can't wait to share them with you!

Thank You for Reading!

We hope you and your little ones have enjoyed the adventures of Max and their friends in our Little Yogi series. Your feedback means the world to us, and we would be truly grateful if you could take a moment to share your thoughts by leaving a review.

Your review helps us enhance our future books and allows other families to embark on this magical journey of yoga, mindfulness, and friendship.

Quick Review Links:
Scan the QR code below for your respective Amazon platform to leave your review:

Amazon.com

Amazon.ca

If you didn't purchase the book through Amazon, please leave a review on the website or platform where you bought it.

From the bottom of our hearts, thank you for your unwavering support. We're thrilled to share more of the Little Yogi's tales with you!

Warmest regards,
S.G. Bloomfield
Author of the Little Yogi series

# Little Mantras for Big Hearts

## Patience:

"Just like the sun, I will rise again tomorrow."

## Connection:

"We are all connected, like the waves of the sea."

## Affirmation:

"I am a bright light, shining every day and night."

## Joy and Happiness:

"Happiness is a choice I make."

## Kindness:

"In every action, I choose kindness."

# YOUR DRAWING SPACE

# YOUR DRAWING SPACE

# YOUR DRAWING SPACE

# YOUR DRAWING SPACE

Max
Max Forest

www.ingramcontent.com/pod-product-compliance
Ingram Content Group UK Ltd.
Pitfield, Milton Keynes, MK11 3LW, UK
UKRC031011310726
14089UKWH00014B/251

* 9 7 8 1 7 3 8 0 2 7 4 1 5 *